The House That Stood on Booker Hill

Written by Cass Hollander
Illustrated by Christa Kieffer

The house that stood on Booker
Hill was old. It had been on that spot
for about 200 years.

The house on Booker Hill was built
in 1790. It was built by the Hood family.

The man who built the house
worked with his tools. He cut wood for
the roof.

The house looked new in 1790.
The family painted the house white.

The children swept the rooms with a broom. The family made the broom with a stick and straw.

The family sat on the porch to
stay cool in the summer.

The children would jump into the nearby pond. They would swim in the cool pool of water.

The house on Booker Hill started out small. People added rooms in 1840.

At noon, the family would sit around
a table. The mother cooked a big dinner.
She used black pots and wooden spoons
when she cooked.

Sometimes she cooked a goose. There
was lots of good food to go with it.

1890

The family who lived in the house
on Booker Hill raised the roof in 1890.
The house got bigger.

The children played in front of the house. They rolled their hoops. Their hoops were made of wood.

The children would carry their books
to school. It was a long walk.

Their dog would snooze in the
sun. It would wait for the children to
come home from school.

1940

The family who lived in the house
on Booker Hill in 1940 liked plants.
They planted lots of flowers and trees.

They planted a rosebush. The
rosebush bloomed every year.

The children loved the little room at
the top of the house. They would play in
that room.

They would read books there, too.

1990

The bride and groom stood on the porch of the house. They looked at their new house.

They looked at the rooms.

The house that stood on Booker Hill
had a new family again.